SPACE SCIENCE

EARTH

BY BETSY RATHBURN

BELLWETHER MEDIA • MINNEAPOLIS, MN

TM

Are you ready to take it to the extreme? Torque books thrust you into the action-packed world of sports, vehicles, mystery, and adventure. These books may include dirt, smoke, fire, and chilling tales. **WARNING**: read at your own risk.

This edition first published in 2019 by Bellwether Media, Inc.

No part of this publication may be reproduced in whole or in part without written permission of the publisher.
For information regarding permission, write to Bellwether Media, Inc.,
Attention: Permissions Department,
6012 Blue Circle Drive, Minnetonka, MN 55343.

Library of Congress Cataloging-in-Publication Data

Names: Rathburn, Betsy, author.
Title: Earth / by Betsy Rathburn.
Description: Minneapolis, MN : Bellwether Media, Inc., [2019] | Series:
   Torque. Space Science | Audience: Ages 7-12. | Audience: Grades 3 to 7. |
   Includes bibliographical references and index.
Identifiers: LCCN 2018039180 (print) | LCCN 2018040544 (ebook) | ISBN
   9781681036892 (ebook) | ISBN 9781626179714 (hardcover : alk. paper)
Subjects: LCSH: Earth (Planet)–Juvenile literature.
Classification: LCC QB631.4 (ebook) | LCC QB631.4 .R375 2019 (print) | DDC
   525–dc23
LC record available at https://lccn.loc.gov/2018039180

Editor: Kate Moening   Designer: Andrea Schneider

Printed in the United States of America, North Mankato, MN.

TABLE OF CONTENTS

LONG-DISTANCE SELFIE

It is February 14, 1990. After 13 years of traveling, *Voyager 1* is 3.7 billion miles (6 billion kilometers) from Earth. The spacecraft turns toward Earth to take one last photo before its cameras shut down.

The photo shows bands of color on a dark background. In one band, Earth is a pale blue dot. This long-distance selfie is one of the most famous photos in the world!

FUN FACT

WORLD-FAMOUS WORDS

A scientist named Carl Sagan had the idea to take the famous *Voyager 1* photo. He gave a popular speech in which he called Earth a "pale blue dot." People remember his words more than 20 years later!

Voyager 1
"pale blue dot"
photo

WHAT IS EARTH?

Earth is a rocky planet that is about 24,900 miles (40,073 kilometers) around at its **equator**. The equator is an imaginary line that circles Earth at its widest point.

Earth is the fifth-largest planet in the solar system! It is a mostly round globe with flattened **poles**. The poles are angled so that Earth's **axis** is tilted.

EARTH'S POLES

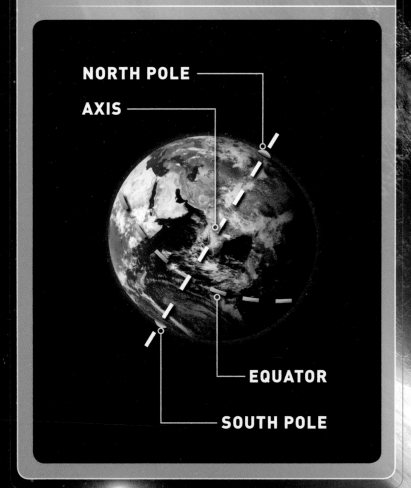

NORTH POLE

AXIS

EQUATOR

SOUTH POLE

FUN FACT

WHAT A BLAST!

Melted rocks in the upper mantle create a hot material called magma. It comes out of Earth's crust as lava!

Earth's center is an inner **core** made of the metals iron and nickel. A liquid metal outer core surrounds it.

Beyond the outer core is the **mantle**. This thick layer is made of melted hot metals and **minerals**. Earth's **crust** surrounds the mantle. Humans live on the crust's rocky surface!

EARTH'S LAYERS

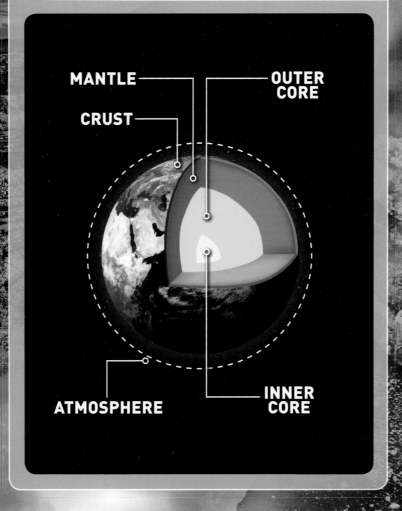

MANTLE

CRUST

OUTER CORE

ATMOSPHERE

INNER CORE

Earth is surrounded by an **atmosphere**. This is made up mostly of the gases nitrogen and oxygen. The atmosphere warms Earth by trapping heat from the Sun. It also keeps the planet from overheating.

The atmosphere protects Earth from **meteorites**. It burns them up before they reach Earth's surface! The atmosphere even affects weather. Without it, Earth would not have wind or rain!

METEORITES

HOW DID EARTH FORM?

Earth began to form about 4.6 billion years ago. **Gravity** pulled together a huge cloud of gas and dust. This became the Sun. Leftover pieces circled around it.

Eventually, these pieces grouped together and grew larger. After millions of years, one group of pieces became Earth. The planet had just the right gases and temperatures to host life!

ILLUSTRATION OF
SOLAR SYSTEM FORMING

Many years after it formed, Earth was struck by a huge rock. The **impact** threw more rocks into space. Scientists believe these materials formed the Moon!

Today, the Moon is important to life on Earth. Its gravity keeps Earth steady as it spins through space. It also affects the ocean's **tides**.

WHERE IS EARTH FOUND?

Earth is the third-closest planet to the Sun. It is about 93 million miles (150 million kilometers) away. Only Mercury and Venus are closer!

The solar system is made up of planets that **orbit** the Sun. Earth completes one orbit about once every 365 days. This makes a year. As Earth orbits, it also spins on its axis. This creates day and night!

FUN FACT

LEAP YEAR

Earth orbits the Sun once every 365.25 days. Because of this, an extra day is added every four years. Leap years add February 29 to the calendar!

WHY DO WE STUDY EARTH?

Scientists use spacecraft called **satellites** to study Earth. These machines orbit Earth to take pictures and collect information.

Satellites help scientists keep track of changes on Earth. They may spot wildfires or pollution problems. They also look at weather patterns and changes in sea levels. The information helps scientists solve problems!

FUN FACT

MESSAGE IN A BOTTLE

Voyagers 1 and *2* are famous for carrying the Golden Record. This record is full of sounds and pictures from Earth. It is a message to other life forms that may one day find it!

INTERNATIONAL SPACE
STATION SATELLITE

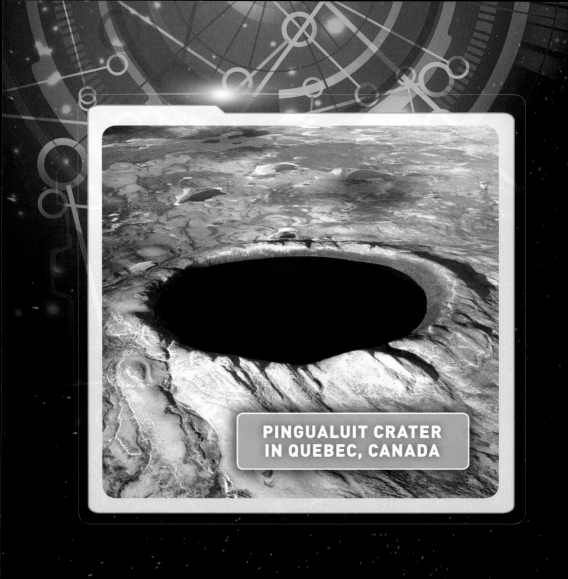

PINGUALUIT CRATER
IN QUEBEC, CANADA

Studying Earth also helps scientists study
other planets. Earth's rocks and **craters** give
clues to how other planets may have formed.

If scientists know how water and life formed on Earth, they can look for the same signs on other planets. Studying Earth helps humans explore space!

GLOSSARY

atmosphere–the gases that surround Earth and other planets

axis–the invisible line around which Earth rotates

core–the innermost part of Earth

craters–deep holes in the surface of an object

crust–the outermost part of Earth's surface

equator–an imaginary circle around a star or planet that is equal distance from each pole

gravity–the force that pulls objects toward one another

impact–an event in which objects hit one another

mantle–the layer of Earth below the crust and above the outer core

meteorites–pieces of asteroids that make it through Earth's atmosphere

minerals–naturally occurring substances found in rocks, sands, and soils

orbit–to move around something in a fixed path

poles–either end of a planet or star; every planet or star has two poles.

satellites–objects that orbit planets and asteroids

tides–the rise and fall of the oceans that occurs twice a day on Earth

TO LEARN MORE

AT THE LIBRARY

Goldstein, Margaret J. *Discover Earth*. Minneapolis, Minn.: Lerner Publications, 2018.

Nandi, Ishani, ed. *First Space Encyclopedia*. New York, N.Y.: DK Publishing, 2016.

Riggs, Kate. *Planets*. Mankato, Minn.: Creative Education, 2015.

ON THE WEB

FACTSURFER

Factsurfer.com gives you a safe, fun way to find more information.

1. Go to www.factsurfer.com.

2. Enter "Earth" into the search box.

3. Click the "Surf" button and select your book cover to see a list of related web sites.

INDEX

The images in this book are reproduced through the courtesy of: robert_s, front cover, p. 2; MSFC/ NASA Images, pp. 4-5; NASA/Voyager 1/ Wikipedia, p. 5 (inset); ixpert, p. 7; Roberto Destarac Photo, pp. 8-9; Oliver Denker, pp. 10-11; NASA/JPL-Caltech/ NASA Images, pp. 12-13; Mopic, p. 15 (Earth); ifong, pp. 14-15 (rocks); Vadim Sadovski, pp. 16-17; xtock, pp. 18-19 (Earth); Nerthuz, pp. 18-19 (ISS); NASA/ Denis Sarrazin/ Wikipedia, p. 20; Fisherss, p. 21 (Earth); taffpixture, p. 21 (Moon).